'Word To The Wise'

Table of Contents

Introduction

This work is intended as a journey through quotes and pearls of wisdom.

The quotes are from an array of sources and varying cultures, for wisdom does not belong to any one tribe of people.

Indeed, wisdom is not always appreciated in these modern times, where it is apparent that materialism and its incessant tenant of instant gratification are taken as the order of the day by many.

Two quotes of the famous author George Orwell come to mind 'The further a society drifts from truth the more it will hate those who speak it.'

And,

'In a time of universal deceit - telling the truth is a revolutionary act.'

It is not a sombre project, for indeed, much wisdom relates to the heart and spiritual welfare of creation. Thus, we start our journey with the following quote that summarizes our vision.

'Certain things catch your eye, but pursue only those that capture the heart.'
Ancient Indian Proverb

'What you find depends on how you seek.'

Abu Ayyub

'Indeed, actions are by their intention.'

Prophet Muhammad ﷺ

'Waste no more time arguing about what a good man should be. Be one.'

Marcus Aurelius

'When you arise in the morning think of what a privilege it is to be alive, to think, to enjoy, to love...'

Marcus Aurelius

'Dwell on the beauty of life. Watch the stars, and see yourself running with them.'

Marcus Aurelius

'It is not death that a man should fear, but he should fear never beginning to live.'

Marcus Aurelius

'When I was 5 years old, my mother always told me that happiness was the key to life. When I went to school, they asked me what I wanted to be when I grew up. I wrote down 'happy'. They told me I didn't understand the assignment, and I told them they didn't understand life.'

John Lennon

'The soul becomes dyed with the colour of its thoughts.'

Marcus Aurelius

'You have power over your mind - not outside events. Realize this, and you will find strength.'

Marcus Aurelius

'Don't confuse humility with weakness, nor weakness with humility, although often weakness leads to humility.'

Abu Ayyub

'We can easily forgive a child who is afraid of the dark; the real tragedy of life is when men are afraid of the light.'

Plato

'The best revenge is to be unlike him who performed the injury.'

Marcus Aurelius

'Wise men speak because they have something to say; fools because they have to say something.'

Plato

'Nothing will work unless you do.'

Maya Angelou

'I alone cannot change the world, but I can cast a stone across the water to create many ripples.'

Mother Teresa

'What we achieve inwardly will change our outer reality.'

Plutarch

'Be the change you want to see in the world.'

Many
Attributed to Gandhi (said in other words)
Arleen Lorrance and others.

'Indeed, Allah will not change the condition of a people
until they change what is within themselves.'
The Sacred Qur'an 13:11

'How much time he gains who does not look to see what his neighbour says or does or thinks, but only at what he does himself, to make it just and holy.'

Marcus Aurelius

'Do not act as if you were going to live ten thousand years. Death hangs over you. While you live, while it is in your power, be good.'

Marcus Aurelius

'When I hear somebody sigh, 'Life is hard,' I am always tempted to ask, compared to what?'

Sydney Harris

'Everything has beauty, but not everyone can see.'

Confucius

'If it is not right do not do it; if it is not true do not say it.'

Marcus Aurelius

'Never let the future disturb you. You will meet it, if you have to, with the same weapons of reason which today arm you against the present.'

Marcus Aurelius

'Do not get angry! Do not get angry!
Do not get angry!'[1]

Prophet Muhammad ﷺ

'How much more grievous are the consequences of anger
than the causes of it[2].'

Marcus Aurelius

---

[1] What is meant here is do not choose to be angry, or act out of anger, especially for ones own sake.

[2] This is in general of course, as for grotesque and barbaric ethnic cleansing, apartheid and holocausts, anger seldom boils into greater crimes.

'Anybody can become angry — that is easy, but to be angry with the right person and to the right degree and at the right time and for the right purpose, and in the right way — that is not within everybody's power and is not easy.'

Aristotle

'Whenever you are about to find fault with someone, ask yourself the following question: What fault of mine most nearly resembles the one I am about to criticise?'

Marcus Aurelius

'The best revenge is to be unlike your enemy.'

Marcus Aurelius

'Here is a rule to remember in future, when anything tempts you to feel bitter: not 'This is misfortune,' but 'To bear this worthily is good fortune'.'

Marcus Aurelius

'Gracious, beautiful patience is most befitting[3].'

Chapter Joseph of The Sacred Qur'an 12:18 and 12:83

'So, persevere with beautiful patience.'

The Sacred Qur'an 70:4

'Your periods of suffering and difficulty can teach you lessons you will not learn anywhere else.'

Attaullah

---

[3] It is the most gracious, beautiful and noble of course of action to take when a bitter event transpires. How beautiful is comely perseverance, this was the statement of prophet Jacob.

'O you who believe, seek help through prayer and patience. Indeed, Allah is with those who persevere.'

The Sacred Qur'an 2:153

'Whoever would be patient, then Allah will make him patient. There is no gift that is better and more comprehensive than patience.'[4]

The Prophet Muhammad ﷺ

---

[4] From a longer quote 'The Prophet said, "**If I had anything, I would not withhold it. Whoever refrains from asking others, then Allah will make him content. Whoever would be independent, then Allah will make him independent. Whoever would be patient, then Allah will make him patient. There is no gift that is better and more comprehensive than patience.**' The narration is Authentic and is found in Bukhari and Muslim.

'True richness is contentment of the heart.'

The Prophet Muhammad ﷺ

'The most priceless thing in this world is peace of mind.'

Anon

'Begin, be bold, and venture to be wise.'

Horace

'It is the mark of an educated mind to be able to entertain a thought without accepting it.'

Aristotle

'Do not make your heart like a sponge that soaks up whatever is put in front of it...'

Ibn Taymiyyah[5]

---

[5] Ibn Taymiyyah said this to his student Ibn Qayyim

'Although I'm only fourteen, I know quite well what I want, I know who is right and who is wrong. I have my opinions, my own ideas and principles, and although it may sound pretty mad from an adolescent, I feel more of a person than a child, I feel quite independent of anyone.'

Anne Frank

'Educating the mind without educating the heart is no education at all.'

Aristotle

'Excellence is never an accident. It is always the result of high intention, sincere effort, and intelligent execution; it represents the wise choice of many alternatives - choice, not chance, determines your destiny.'

Aristotle

'Patience is bitter, but its fruit is sweet.'

Aristotle

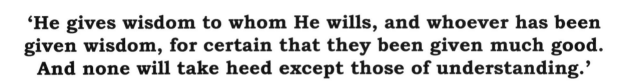

'He gives wisdom to whom He wills, and whoever has been given wisdom, for certain that they been given much good. And none will take heed except those of understanding.'

The Sacred Qur'an 2:269

'Perseverance is half of faith...'

Abdullaah bin Masood as quoted by
Ibn Al Qayyim

'...and half is being grateful.'

Abdullaah bin Masood

'He who is not contented with what he has, would not be contented with what he would like to have.'

Socrates

'Outright reject the idea that you have to be constantly working, toiling in order to be successful. Embrace the concept that rest, recovery & reflection are fundamental parts of the process and progress towards a successful contented life, contentment is more valuable than material success.'

Based on a number of quotes

'Don't look at those with more with you but recall those who have been favoured with less.'

The Prophet Muhammad ﷺ

'Not every opponent you fight is your enemy and not all those who help you are your friends.'

Mike Tyson

'A friend to all is a friend to none.'

Aristotle

'Learn to light a candle in the darkest moments of someone's life. Be the light that helps others see; it is what gives life its deepest significance.'

Roy T. Bennett

'Gentleness is never in something except that it adds to it, harshness is never in something except that it spoils it.'

The Prophet Muhammad ﷺ

'Those who are merciful will be shown mercy by the Most Merciful. Be merciful to those on the earth and the One in the heaven will be merciful to you.'[6]

The Prophet Muhammad ﷺ

---

[6] The narration is authentic. - [At-Tirmidhi]

'Whoever does not show mercy will not be shown mercy.'[7]

The Prophet Muhammad ﷺ

'We do not call it warming the heart and breaking the ice without reason, for ice is not melted by adding more ice, so let us focus on warming hearts and being compassionate so that we will be shown compassion.'

Abu Ayyub

---

[7] Authentic narration found in Bukhari and Muslim

'Don't despair of the Mercy of Allah (God), indeed, He forgives all sins, indeed, He is The perpetually Forgiving, The Most Compassionate.'

The Sacred Qur'an 39:53

'If we do not enjoin our people to goodness and call them to leave evil, evil will join us and good will leave us.'

Abu Ayyub

'A wise man can play the part of a fool, but a fool can't play the part of a wise man.'

Adapted from Malcolm X

'Be patient over what they say and avoid them with a gracious avoidance.'

The Sacred Qur'an 73:10

'Those who know, do. Those that understand, teach.'

Aristotle

'Stand for the truth or fall for a lie'

Abu Ayyub

'If you don't stand for something you will fall for anything.'

Malcolm X

'The educated differ from the uneducated as much as the living differ from the dead.'

Aristotle

'You're not supposed to be so blind with patriotism that you can't face reality. Wrong is wrong, no matter who says it.'

Malcolm X

'I have more respect for a man who lets me know where he stands, even if he's wrong, than the one who comes up like an angel and is nothing but a devil.'

Malcolm X

'I count him braver who overcomes his desires than him who conquers his enemies, for the hardest victory is over self.'

Aristotle

Someone said, "What is the greater jihad?" He said: "The servant's struggle against his self."

Attributed to the prophet Muhammad ﷺ [8]

---

[8] Whilst this narration is disputed in terms of authenticity there is a supporting authentic narration on the following page that supports the same meaning.

'The one who strives (literally makes jihad) **in the way of Allah the Exalted is he who strives against his soul.'**

Prophet Muhammad ﷺ [9] [10]

9

Source: Musnad Ahmad 23445, Grade: *Sahih*

Sunan al-Tirmidhī 1621

Grade: *Sahih* (authentic) according to Al-Tirmidhi

[10] Ibn Qayyim reported: It was said to Hasan Al-Basri, "O Abu Sa'eed, which jihad is best?" Hasan, may Allah have mercy on him, said:

Your jihad against your desires. Rawdat Al-Muhibeen 1/478

'I never dealt with anything more difficult on me than my own self. Sometimes it would be against me, and sometimes it would be for me.'

Sufyan al-Thawri

'Indeed, triumphant (in eternal success), is he who had purified her (the soul) and indeed, ruined is he who had corrupted her.'

The Sacred Qur'an 91:9-10

'You may not agree with me but if you speak to me in a nice way I may just listen to you and change my opinion.'

Muhammad Robert heft

'I believe in human beings, and that all human beings should be respected as such, regardless of their colour.'

Malcolm X

'If you form the habit of taking what someone else says about a thing without checking it out for yourself, you'll find that other people will have you hating your friends and loving your enemies.'

Malcolm X

'Mankind what is wrong with you that you do not help each other? What is wrong with you they you do not help the animals and plant life? Do you not know that we are responsible for our condition?'

Abu ayyub

'Help others if you want to be helped.'

'If you want to be happy, strive to make others happy.'[11]

Abu Ayyub

'The more people you make happy the happier you will be.'

Muslim Belal

---

[11] Helping those in need survive with essentials is a far more important matter than helping those who are not in dire need with creature comforts.

'Pleasure in the job puts perfection in the work.'

Aristotle

"The purpose of life is not to be happy. It is to be useful, to be honourable, to be compassionate, to have it make some difference that you have lived and lived well."

Ralph Waldo Emerson

'There is no exercise better for the heart than reaching down and lifting people up.'

John Holmes

'Remember this. Hold on to this. This is the only perfection there is, the perfection of helping others. This is the only thing we can do that has any lasting meaning. This is why we're here. To make each other feel safe.'

Andre Agassi

'When you reach out to those in need, do not be surprised if the essential meaning of something occurs.'

Stephen Richards

'Help others and give something back. I guarantee you will discover that while public service improves the lives and the world around you, its greatest reward is the enrichment and new meaning it will bring your own life.'
Arnold Schwarzenegger

'Service to humanity is service to God.'

Lailah Gifty Akita

"The service you do for others is the rent you pay for your room here on Earth."

Muhammad Ali

'What we have done for ourselves alone dies with us; what we have done for others and the world remains and is immortal.'

Albert Pike

'You need an attitude of service. You're not just serving yourself. You help others to grow up and you grow with them.'

David Green

'The work an unknown good man has done is like a vein of water flowing hidden underground, secretly making the ground green.'

Thomas Carlyle

'Earn your success based on service to others not at the expense of others.'

H. Jackson Brown Jr.

'No one is useless in this world who lightens the burdens of another.'

Charles Dickens

'When one is helping another, both gain in strength.'

Ecuadorean proverb

'Let's live helping each other in this world.'

Japanese proverb

'Preventing someone from falling is better than helping him get up.'

Italian proverb

'The best place to find a helping hand is at the end of your own arm.'

Swedish proverb

'If you are bitter at heart, sugar in the mouth will not help you.'

Yiddish Proverb

'If you want happiness for an hour — take a nap. If you want happiness for a day — go fishing. If you want happiness for a month — get married. If you want happiness for a year — inherit a fortune. If you want happiness for a lifetime — help someone else.'

Chinese Proverb

'Whoever does not help himself cannot help others.'

Yemeni Proverb

'He who helps little, gets little help.'

J.G.R

'Never worry about numbers. Help one person at a time, and always start with the person nearest to you.'

Mother Teresa

'And what can make you know what the steep path is?
It is: Freeing a slave, Or feeding (those in need) on a day of
severe hunger
An orphan near in relation (or location) , Or someone
destitute (literally the one of dust, who only owns dust) then
(thereafter) he was of those who called people with wisdom
to patience and invited them (with wisdom) to merciful
conduct Those are are the companions of the right.'

The Sacred Qur'an 90:11-18

'If someone helps others,
Allah will send others to help him, by His grace.'

Abu Ayyub

'A willing helper does not wait until he is asked.'

Danish Proverb

'If the horse is already dead more hay will not help it.'

Filipino Proverb

'Men will not be fortunate without a helping hand from misfortune.'

Russian Proverb

'Amazing is the affair of the believer, verily all of his affair is good and this is not for no one except the believer. If something of good/happiness befalls him he is grateful and that is good for him. If something of harm befalls him he is patient and that is good for him.'[12]

The Prophet Muhammad

---

[12] The narration is authentic and is found in the collection of Muslim.

'At times one needs to help oneself to get to a safe place, to a ridge or peak first before they can cast the rope down to help others, as one may be able to boost others but fall themselves, whereas if they climb and better themselves (at times) they can survive and help many more...'

Abu Ayyub

'You cannot force others to take the help they need.'

J.G.R

'It is right that one cannot sleep if there is a cat or dog outside dying without essential provision, it is even more important if ones fellow man is left without the essentials, and the most important of essentials in truth is spiritual knowledge, the sacred knowledge that ensures ones eternal survival and wellbeing.'

Abu Ayyub

'May your charity increase as much as your wealth..'

Eskimo Proverb.

'Wealth of a man is not diminished by giving in charity.'

The Prophet Muhammad

'Better to light a candle than curse the darkness.'

Chinese Proverb

'There is no pillow so soft as a clear conscience.'

French Proverb

'A bird that you set free may be caught again, but a word that escapes your lips will not return.'

Jewish Proverb

'If you guarantee me that which in-between your legs and that which in-between your jaws I will guarantee you paradise.'

The Prophet Muhammad

'If you don't want anyone to find out, don't do it.'

Chinese Proverb

'A joke is often a hole through which truth whistles.'

Japanese Proverb

'A mother understands what a child does not say.'

Jewish Proverb

'If you are going to walk on thin ice, you might as well dance..'

Eskimo Proverb.

'Do not stand in a place of danger trusting in miracles.'

African Proverb

'**If you have no shame** (about a matter) **do what you wish.**'

The Prophet Muhammad

'A pretty face and fine clothes do not make character.'

Congolese Proverb

'Don't bargain for fish that are still in the water.'

Indian Proverb

'He who wants a rose must respect the thorn.'

Persian Proverb

'If you want to build high, you must dig deep.'

Mongolian Proverb

'Better to ask the way than go astray.'

Korean Proverb

Sunshine all the time makes a desert.

Arab Proverb

Beware the person with nothing to lose.

Italian Proverb

Patience is bitter but it bears sweet fruit.

Turkish Proverb

'If you speak too much, you will learn too little.'

Armenian Proverb

'A fool says what he knows, and a wise man knows what he says.'

Yiddish Proverb

'A donkey carrying a pile of holy books is still a donkey.'[13]

Far Eastern Proverb

---

[13] This is like the parable in the Qur'an, **''The example of those who were burdened with the Torah, but then did not carry it, is like a donkey carrying books. Evil is the example of the people which deny the signs of God, and God does not guide the wrongdoing people.'. The Sacred Qurʾān 62:5** *A donkey can carry books but not act on the guidance within the sacred pages, man can, but when they choose not to after memorising the divine guidance, they are worse than an ass.*

'Do not judge by appearances, a rich heart may be under a poor coat.'

Scottish Proverb

'Sharp acids corrode their own containers.'

Albanian Proverb

'Resentment is like drinking poison and then hoping it will kill your enemies.'

Nelson Mandela

'It is difficult to steal when the boss is a thief.'

Icelandic Proverb

'A hungry wolf is stronger than a satisfied dog.'

Ukranian Proverb

'When the character of a man is not clear to you, look at his friends.'

Japanese Proverb

'Tell me who your friends are, so I can tell you who you are.'

Bulgarian Proverb

'Be careful who you take as a close friend for you are upon the way of life of your companions.'

Prophet Muhammad ﷺ

'He that is unkind to his own will not be kind to others.'

Galician Proverb

'There is no shame in not knowing, the shame lies in not finding out.'

Russian Proverb

'He who buys what he does not need steals from himself.'

Swedish Proverb

'He who begins many things finishes few.'

German Proverb

'What an old man can see while seated, a young man cannot see standing.'

Eritrean Proverb

'Who is wise? One who learns from every man... Who is strong? One who overpowers his inclinations... Who is rich? One who is satisfied with his lot... Who is honorable? One who honors his fellows.'

Ben Zoma, Ethics of the Fathers, 4:1

'Wisdom does not belong exclusively to any single tribe, nor is it held exclusively by mankind, what is incumbent on the discerning is to take heed of the statements and lessons of benefit, for otherwise it is a disservice to the God given intellect He has blessed you with.'

J.G.R

'I'm for truth, no matter who tells it. I'm for justice, no matter who it is for or against. I'm a human being, first and foremost, and as such I'm for whoever and whatever benefits humanity as a whole.'

Malcolm X

"I don't stand for the black man's side, I don't stand for the white man's side. I stand for God's side"

Bob Marley

'Education is the passport to the future, for tomorrow belongs to those who prepare for it today.'

Malcolm X

'Through discipline comes freedom.'

Aristotle

'The aim of art is to represent not the outward appearance of things, but their inward significance.'

Aristotle

'One of the first things I think young people, especially nowadays, should learn is how to see for yourself and listen for yourself and think for yourself. Then you can come to an intelligent decision for yourself. If you form the habit of going by what you hear others say about someone, or going by what others think about someone, instead of searching that thing out for yourself and seeing for yourself, you will be walking west when you think you're going east, and you will be walking east when you think you're going west.'

Malcolm X

'You can't separate peace from freedom because no one can be at peace unless he has his freedom.'

Malcolm X

'We make war that we may live in peace.'[14]

Aristotle

'It is not always the same thing to be a good man and a good citizen.'

Aristotle

---

[14] Peace of any kind including peace of mind is only found by hard work, if there are violent forces they will not cease until they are striven against.

'Freedom is not freedom of desires but true freedom is from free from being a slave to one's desires.'[15]

Abu Ayyub

'Live and learn or live and burn.'[16]

Abu Ayyub

'The high-minded man must care more for the truth than for what people think.'

Aristotle

---

[15] Having ones desires dictate ones actions all of the time means there is no difference between such a person and a beast, rather being able which desire to entertain is when one is no longer a slave to the caprices of the soul, and when they entertain such, it should be in the context of a desire that does not oppose the lofty goal of the eternal success of the soul.

[16] **Whether in this world or the next if we do not fix our ways when we make errors we will pay for our own choices.**

'The antidote for fifty enemies is one friend.'

Aristotle

'A sin can lead to paradise and a good deed can lead to fire.'

Ibn Al Qayyim and others

'Put God first!'

Denzel Washington

'Hard work...works!'

Denzel Washington

'Hard work beats talent - when talent doesn't work hard!'

'Success is sweet but the secret is sweat.'

Norman Schwarzkopf Jr.

'No one can teach, if by teaching we mean the transmission of knowledge, in any mechanical fashion, from one person to another. The most that can be done is that one person who is more knowledgeable than another can, by asking a series of questions, stimulate the other to think, and so cause him to learn for himself.[17]

Socrates

'That person who seeks divine knowledge to attain the material world finds that such knowledge has no place in his heart.'

Imam Abu Hanifa

'Difficulties are the result of sin (mistakes). The sinful therefore does not have the right to lament when difficulties befall him.'

Imam Abu Hanifa

---

[17] In essence one cannot force someone to comprehend or truly learn any given thing, one cannot force feed wisdom.

'A little action with knowledge is far more beneficial than a lot of action with ignorance.'

Imam Abu Hanifa

'Knowledge without deeds is like body without soul. As long as knowledge doesn't embrace the existence of action it will not be enough not agreeable nor sincere.'

Imam Abu Hanifa

'Once a man asked Imam Abu Hanifa: 'O Imam! When I take a bath in the river, should I face the direction of prayer or turn away from the direction of praye?'
Then Imam replied, 'If I were you, I would face my clothes, to make sure that no one runs off with them.'

Imam Abu Hanifa

'Pointing at others is most often pointless, the moral of the story is point-less.'

Abu Ayyub

'The memory is the scribe of the soul'

Aristotle

'Often when we generalise, we tell general-lies'

Abu Ayyub

'Leave what makes you doubt for what doesn't make you doubt.'

The Prophet Muhammad ﷺ

'Better safe than sorry!'

British Proverb

'The situation will not change till we change what is within ourselves.'

Abu Ayyub's reflection on The Sacred Qur'an 13:11

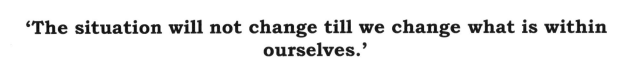

'Indeed, with hardship is ease.'

The Sacred Qur'an 94:6

'A persons' tongue can give you the taste of His heart.'

Ibn Al Qayyim

'Knowledge will bring honour to you in this world and the hereafter.'

Sufyan ath-Thawree

'When you do not have knowledge someone can bring you dirt and you will believe it is gold.'

Ibn Al Qayyim

'We must be neither cowardly nor rash but courageous.'
Aristotle

'And tire yourself out, because it makes life worth living! I have seen that water stagnates when it stands still, yet when it runs it is sweet and pure.'

Imam Shafi

'Be truthful at all times and in all places. Stay away from lying and deception, and do not sit alongside liars and deceivers, for all such deeds are sins.'

Sufyan al-Thawri

'Whoever's knowledge makes themselves cry, that person is the true scholar.'

Sufyan al-Thawri

'The most difficult thing I keep observing is my intentions as it is always apt to change.'

Sufyan al-Thawri

'Spread your knowledge, but be careful of popularity.'[18]

Sufyan al-Thawri

---

[18] The reason to be cautious of fame is that it is indeed a poisoned chalice, one can set off with good intentions but become corrupted in the limelight.

'Three qualities are from perseverance:

[1]Not speaking about your misfortune.
[2]Not talking about your pain.
[3]Not praising yourself'.'

Sufyan al-Thawri

'If **Shaytaan** (the devil) **defeated me yesterday, I will defeat him today with repentance and good deeds.'**

Sufyan al-Thawri

'Be **patient at all times and in all places, for patience leads to righteousness and righteousness leads to paradise. Do not** (choose to) **become angry and furious for these two emotions lead to wickedness, and wickedness leads to the Hellfire.'**

Imam Sufyan ath-Thawri

'Indeed, these kings have abandoned the hereafter for you, so leave the world for them.'

Sufyan Al-Thawri

'Render unto Caesar the things that are Caesar's, and unto God the things that are God's.'

Matthew 21:22

'Keep yourself busy in remembering your faults, so that you have no time left to remember the fault of others.'

Sufyan al-Thawri

'If you know yourself, then you'll not be harmed by what is said about you.'

Sufyan al-Thawri

'God is One
The eternal king of refuge
He was not born nor were any born from Him
There is no comparison unto Him
The Sacred Qur'an 112

'Do not despair or the mercy of Allah.'

The Sacred Qur'an 39:53

'Do not despair of the relief from Allah.'

The Sacred Qur'an 12:87

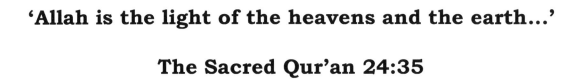

'Allah is the light of the heavens and the earth...'

The Sacred Qur'an 24:35

'Not one of you is a true believer until he loves for people that which he loves for himself.'

The Prophet Muhammad ﷺ

'True wisdom comes to each of us when we realize how little we understand about life, ourselves, and the world around us.'

Socrates

'Awareness of ignorance is the beginning of wisdom.'

Socrates

'Speak good or remain silent.'

The Prophet Muhammad ﷺ

'When the debate is lost, slander becomes the tool of the loser.'

Socrates

'Study the past if you would define the future.'

Confusious

'No pain - no gain!'

'He who learns but does not think is lost! He who thinks but does not learn is in great danger.'

Confusious

'Ignorance is the night of the mind, but a night without moon and star.'[19]

Confusious

---

[19] This quote goes some way to explaining why 'ignorance can be bliss' because it causes the soul to be in a form of ease, although temporary, being spiritually blind means one cannot see the issue at hand, for a night without stars is useless to a traveller...

'Be in this world as a traveller.'

The Prophet Muhammad ﷺ

'Don't believe everything you hear...'

'If you give a man a fish, you will feed him for a day. Teach a man to fish, you will feed him for a lifetime.'

Confusious

'Our greatest glory is not in never falling, but in rising every time we fall.'

Confucius

'If you want to be wrong then follow the masses.'

Socrates

'You will never be able to please everyone, rather rectify what is between you and God Almighty and do not care about the people (say in that regard).'

Imam Shafi

.

'A leader leads by example, not by force.'

Sun Tzu

'If you know the enemy and know yourself, you need not fear the result of a hundred battles. If you know yourself but not the enemy, for every victory gained you will also suffer a defeat. If you know neither the enemy nor yourself, you will succumb in every battle.'

Sun Tzu

'Supreme excellence consists of breaking the enemy's resistance without fighting.'

Sun Tzu

'You have to believe in yourself.'

Sun Tzu

'Fools are those who debate the ignorant.'

Imam Shafi

'Always hate what is wrong, but don't hate the one who errors. Hate sin with all your heart, but forgive and have mercy on the sinner. Criticize speech, but respect the speaker. Our job is to wipe out disease, not the patient.' –

Imam Shafi

'If you are on the way towards Allah, then run. if it's hard for you then jog: even crawl, but never stop or go back.' –

Imam Shafi

'If people reflected upon Surah Al-Asr, it would be sufficient for them (as a lesson).'

Imam Shafi

'By time, verily mankind are in loss, except for those who believe and do righteous works , and advise one another with wisdom to the truth and advise one another with wisdom to steadfastness.'

The Sacred Qur'an 103:1-3

Imam al-Shafi'i remarked, 'There is a verse in the Quran that every wrongdoer should be terrified of.' He was asked, 'Which verse is that?'
"And your Lord never forgets" He replied.'

The Sacred Qur'an 19:64

'To admonish your brother in private is to advise him and improve him. But to admonish him publicly is to disgrace and shame him.'

Imam Shafi

Imam Shafi'i was asked why he carried a cane even though he was healthy. He replied,

'To remind myself that I'm a traveller.'

'Be critical[20] of yourself, easy on others.'

Imam Shafi'i

---

[20] If you are going to be hard or critical of anyone then look at yourself, but you should also know that blaming yourself too much is also blameworthy.

'Make life more than just the experience of death.'

Attullah

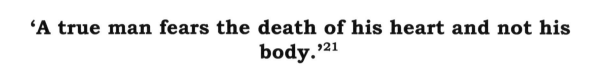

'A true man fears the death of his heart and not his body.'[21]

Ibn Al-Qayyim

---

[21] Thus, the true death of a man is the death of his heart, his faith, his compassion and nobility.

'Despair not from your Lords blessings, If He had wished that you reach the hellfire eternally, He would not have inspired your heart towards Him.'

Imam Shafi'i

'If you don't keep the tongue busy with truth, it will keep you busy with falsehood..'

Imam Shafi'i

'Let not your tongue mention the shame of another, for you yourself are covered in shame and all men have tongues.'

Imam Shafi'i

'Knowledge is not measured by how much is memorized, but rather by how much it is acted on'

Imam Shafi'i

'When the foolish one speaks, do not reply to him, for better than a response (to him) is silence, and if you speak to him, you have aided him, and if you left him (with no reply) in extreme sadness he withers.'

Imam Shafi'i

'The more I learn, the more I learn of my ignorance.'

Imam Shafi'i

'Some people have passed away, but their character has kept them alive, others are alive, but their character has killed them.'

Imam Shafi'i

'Knowledge without action is arrogance.'

Imam Shafi'i

'Victorious warriors win first and then go to war, while defeated warriors go to war first and then seek to win.'

Sun Tzu

'Is life a test or is suffering meaningless?'

J.G.R

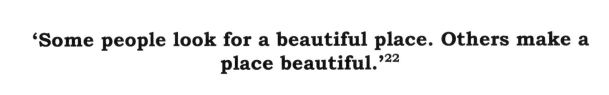

'Some people look for a beautiful place. Others make a place beautiful.'[22]

Inayat khan

---

[22] The following is also true 'Some look for a beautiful place, whilst others look at how to make a place beautiful.'

'Headaches are from the signs of the people of faith and the people of paradise.'

Ibn Rajab

'Life is like riding a bicycle. To keep your balance, you must keep moving.'

Albert Einstein

'He who keeps his own counsel keeps his affairs in his own hands.'

Umar Ibn Al-Khattab[23]

---

[23] Umar Ibn Al-Khattab was a disciple and the 2nd deputy of The Prophet Muhammad

'He who does now know ignorance evil will fall into it.'

Umar Ibn Al-Khattab

'The wisest man is he who can account for his actions.'

Umar Ibn Al-Khattab

'Don't forget your own self while preaching to others.'

Umar Ibn Al-Khattab

'The less of the World, the freer you live.'

Umar Ibn Al-Khattab

'Avoidance of sin is lighter than the pain of remorse.'

Umar Ibn Al-Khattab

'Be patient; for patience is a pillar of faith.'

Umar Ibn Al-Khattab

'Be dignified, honest and truthful.'

Umar Ibn Al-Khattab

'Do not be an arrogant scholar, for scholarship cannot coexist with arrogance.'

Umar Ibn Al-Khattab

'When you see that any scholar loves the world, then his scholarship is in doubt.'

Umar Ibn Al-Khattab

'God forbid, men should be jealous over sacred knowledge as they are jealous over their women.'[24]

Umar Ibn Al-Khattab

---

[24] God forbid that people feel that sacred beneficial knowledge is a prize to be kept for one's self rather than shared with others, especially knowledge that concerns one's eternal safety and wellbeing.

'May Allah bless the man who says less and does more.'

Umar Ibn Al-Khattab

'The criterion of action is that todays work should not be deferred till the following day.'

Umar Ibn Al-Khattab

'Hasten, strive and be quick in the race for forgiveness from your Lord, and for a Garden which width is that (of the entire breadth and expanse) of the heavens and of the earth, prepared for those who pay heed.'

The Sacred Qur'an 3:133

'Luxury is an obstacle, and so is the fatness of the body.'

Umar Ibn Al-Khattab

'A man may be as straight as an arrow, but even then, he will have some critics.'

Umar Ibn Al-Khattab

'O Allah do not give me in excess lest I may be disobedient.'

Umar Ibn Al-Khattab

'Allah loves moderation and hates extravagance and excess.'

Umar Ibn Al-Khattab

'He who went to the kings to seek favours went away from God.'

Umar Ibn Al-Khattab

'Sit with those who love Allah, for that enlightens the mind.'

Umar Ibn Al-Khattab

'If you do ninety-nine things correct, and one thing incorrect, people will ignore the ninety-nine, and spread the one mistake.'

Imam Shafi'i

'Seek help in speech with silence and in reasoning with reflection.'

Imam Shafi'i

'Silence is the best treatment for anger.'

Uthman ibn Affan[25]

---

[25] Uthman Ibn Affan was a disciple and the 3rd deputy of The Prophet Muhammad

'A slip of the tongue is more dangerous than a slip of the feet.'

Uthman ibn Affan

'When a person's tongue becomes quiet and friendly then his heart becomes pious and clean.'

Uthman ibn Affan

'To publicly give charity with an intention to entice people to be charitable is better than giving charity secretly.'

Uthman ibn Affan

'The biggest shame is to mock at something that you have in yourself.'

Ali

Two things define you: Your patience when you have nothing and your attitude when you have everything.

Ali

<u>People</u> act like mirrors; friends reflect your good qualities and enemies your faults.

Ali

'Through patience, great things are accomplished.'

Ali

'If someone is quick in saying about people what they dislike, they speak about him that about which they have no knowledge.'

Ali

'The tongue of the wise man is behind his heart, and the heart of the fool is behind his tongue.'[26]

Ali

---

[26] The fool here follows whatever his tongue says, speaking from his gut, then he puts his heart behind that and does not consult the heart before speaking, as is the case with the wise man.

'The best of riches is the abandonment of (enslavement to) desires.'

Ali

'Some people are so poor all they have is money.'

Various

'Cursed is the man who dies, but the evil done by him survives.'

Abu Bakr As-Sidiq

'Without knowledge action is useless and knowledge without action is futile.'

Abu Bakr As-Sidiq[27]

'Do not trade or deal with an oppressor or his associates.'

Uthman ibn Affan

---

[27] Abu Bakr As-Sidiq The companion and 1st deputy of the Prophet Muhammad ﷺ:

'God blesses him who helps his brother.'

Abu Bakr As-Sidiq

'If you desire blessings from God, be kind to His people.'

Abu Bakr As-Sidiq

'Run away from greatness and greatness will follow you.'

Abu Bakr As-Sidiq[28]

---

28 This does not mean to run away from noble qualities but rather, to run away from fame, for as they say fame is a poisoned chalice, however it at times is a necessary evil, if it is given when one does not covet it for the self, then this is another matter.

'He who avoids complaint, invites happiness.'

Abu Bakr As-Sidiq

'When you count your problems, they seem countless, the solution is to count less,
When you count your blessings they increase manifest, moral is: remember your blessings and you will be more blessed.'

J.G.R

'The secret of happiness, you see, is not found in seeking more, but in developing the capacity to enjoy (one's desires) less.'

Socrates

"If you give thanks I will give you more…"
The Sacred Qur'an 14:7

'If you remember Me, I will remember you Quran.'
The Sacred Qur'an 2:152

'When they ask about Me then I am near.'

The Sacred Qur'an 2:274

'He is The Most Forgiving, The Most Loving.'

The Sacred Qur'an 85:14

'And He is The Most Kind, The Most Aware.'

The Sacred Qur'an 67:14

'Don't count the days make the days count.'

Muhammad Ali

'Friendship is the hardest thing in the world to explain. It's not something you learn in school. But if you haven't learned the meaning of friendship, you really haven't learned anything.'

Muhammad Ali

'Impossible is just a big word thrown around by small men who find it easier to live in the world they've been given than to explore the power they have to change it. Impossible is not a fact. It's an opinion. Impossible is not a declaration. It's a dare. Impossible is potential. Impossible is temporary. Impossible is nothing.'[29]

Muhammad Ali

---

[29] Whilst some things truly are impossible, the self defeatist notion that something possible is impossible is really a false construct and is not anything but negative conjecture in truth

'Champions aren't made in gyms. Champions are made from something they have deep inside them-a desire, a dream, a vision. They have to have the skill, and the will. But the will must be stronger than the skill.'

Muhammad Ali

'I hated every minute of training, but I said, 'Don't quit. Suffer now and live the rest of your life as a champion.'

Muhammad Ali

'Hating people because of their colour is wrong. And it doesn't matter which colour does the hating. It's just plain wrong.'

Muhammad Ali

'The best way to make your dreams come true is to wake up.'

Muhammad Ali

'You have to be asleep to believe the American dream.' [30]

J.G.R

---

[30] The American dream meaning that one can start their own business and thrive is good and positive, however if one means by American dream that materialism is the road to happiness then this is sheer folly.

'Live everyday as if it were your last because someday you're going to be right.'

Muhammad Ali

'The service you do for others is the rent you pay for your room here on Earth.'

Muhammad Ali

'Only a man who knows what it is like to be defeated can reach down to the bottom of his soul and come up with the extra ounce of power it takes to win when the match is even.'

Muhammad Ali

'Silence is golden when you can't think of a good answer.'

Muhammad Ali

'Do not train a child to learn by force or harshness; but direct them to it by what amuses their minds, so that you may be better able to discover with accuracy the peculiar bent of the genius of each.'

Plato

'Life is really simple, but we insist on making it complicated.'

Confucius

'Richness is not in wealth but in contentment of the heart.'

Prophet Muhammad ﷺ

'The secret of happiness, you see, is not found in seeking more, but in developing the capacity to enjoy less.'

Socrates

'Most people, including ourselves, live in a world of relative ignorance. We are even comfortable with that ignorance, because it is all we know. When we first start facing truth, the process may be frightening, and many people run back to their old lives. But if you continue to seek truth, you will eventually be able to handle it better. In fact, you want more! It's true that many people around you now may think you are weird or even a danger to society, but you don't care. Once you've tasted the truth, you won't ever want to go back to being ignorant...'

Socrates

'God does not burden a soul with more than it can bear.'
The Sacred Qur'an 2:286

'I'm not in this world to live up to your expectations and you're not in this world to live up to mine.'

Bruce Lee

'Do not pray for an easy life (of luxury), **pray for the strength to endure a difficult one** (helping others)**.'**

Bruce Lee

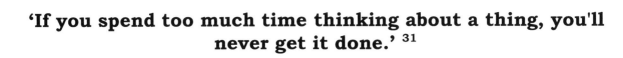

'If you spend too much time thinking about a thing, you'll never get it done.' [31]

Bruce Lee

---

[31] Thus, it is said 'sometimes it is easier done than said...'

'A wise man can learn more from a foolish question than a fool can learn from a wise answer.'

Bruce Lee

'Knowing is not enough, we must apply. Willing is not enough, we must do.'

Bruce Lee

'The doubters said,
'Man can not fly,'
The doers said,
'Maybe, but we'll try,'
And finally soared
In the morning glow
While non-believers
Watched from below.'

Bruce Lee

'Showing off is the fools idea of glory!'

Bruce Lee

'If you don't want to slip up tomorrow, speak the truth today.'

Bruce Lee

'Courage is not the absence of fear but the ability to act in the presence of fear..'

Bruce Lee

'Be careful, however, that the exercise of your rights does not become a stumbling block to the weak.'

1 Corinthians 8:9

'Do not be misled: 'Bad company corrupts good character'.'

1 Corinthians 15:33

'Be careful who you take as a close friend for you are upon the way of life of your companions.'

Prophet Muhammad ﷺ

'Give yourself time.'

Many

'Change your thoughts and you change your world.'

Norman Vincent Peale

'If you want to lift yourself up, lift up someone else.'

Booker T. Washington

'I have learned over the years that when one's mind is made up, this diminishes fear.'

Rosa Parks

'When I stand before God at the end of my life, I would hope that I would not have a single bit of talent left and could say, I used everything you gave me.'

Erma Bombeck

'Do not let any unwholesome talk come out of your mouths, but only what is helpful for building others up according to their needs, that it may benefit those who listen.'

Ephesians 4:29

'Do not forget to show hospitality to strangers, for by so doing some people have shown hospitality to angels without knowing it.'

Hebrews 13:2

'For what shall it profit a man, if he gain the whole world, and suffer the loss of his soul?'

Prophet Jesus

'For everyone who exalts himself will be humbled, and everyone who humbles himself will be exalted.'

Prophet Jesus

'Do not be anxious about tomorrow, for tomorrow will be anxious for itself. Let the day's own trouble be sufficient for the day.'

Prophet Jesus

'The most important thing is to try and inspire people so that they can be great in whatever they want to do.'

Kobe Bryant

'We belong to God, and to Him we will return.'

The Sacred Qur'an 2:156

'So, persevere with a beautiful patience.'

The Sacred Quran 70:4

'You see that people are justified by what they do and not by faith alone.'

James 2:24

'And one of the scribes came up and heard them disputing with one another, and seeing that he answered them well, asked him, 'Which commandment is the most important of all?' Jesus answered, 'The most important is, 'Hear, O Israel: The Lord our God, the Lord is one. And you shall love the Lord your God with all your heart and with all your soul and with all your mind and with all your strength.' The second is this: 'You shall love your neighbour as yourself.' There is no other commandment greater than these.'

Mark 12:28-31

'Good and evil are not equal. Drive away (evil) with what is better, and you will see that the one who there was hostility with, will become like a close friend.'

The Sacred Qur'an 41:34

'O my son establish the Salah (The daily prayers)**, call people to do good and to stop evil deeds. And persevere over whatsoever befalls you** (of trials and calamities) **indeed, this is from the matters that require resolve.** (Steadfastness in patience upon adversity is from the important.)'

Luqman Al Hakeem

The Sacred Qur'an 31:17

'Declare that God is One'

112 The sacred Qur'an

'So where are you going?..'

The sacred Qur'an 81:26

'Every soul shall taste death..'

The sacred Qur'an 3:185

'Guide us to the straight path..'

The Sacred Qur'an 1:5

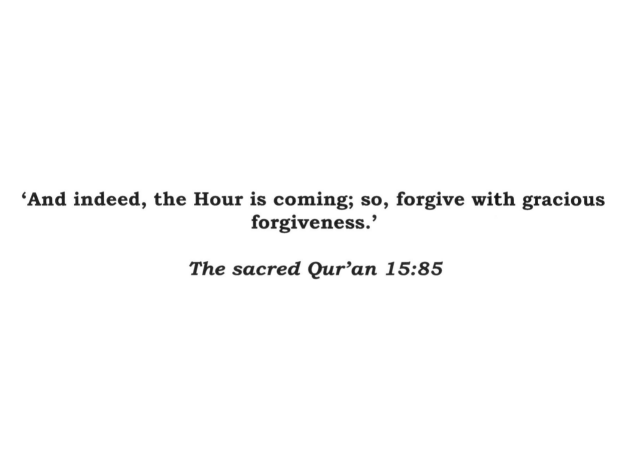

'And indeed, the Hour is coming; so, forgive with gracious forgiveness.'

The sacred Qur'an 15:85

'Practice what you have learned, for theory without practice is like a body without a soul.'

Imam Abu Hanifa

'Is it not in the remembrance of God that hearts find rest?'

The Sacred Qur'an 13:28

'A deprivation of a few moments [of pleasure] is better than permanent regret.'

Ibn Al Qayyim

'Indeed, the mercy of Allah is near to the doers of good.'

The Sacred Qur'an 6:56

'True knowledge is not about profusely narrating but it is about taking heed.'

Ibn al Qayyim

'Indeed, He does not like the arrogant.'

The Sacred Qur'an 16:23

'And the worldly life is not but play and idle diversion; but the home of the hereafter is best for those who are heedful of Allah, so will you not reason?'

The sacred Qur'an 6:32

'Do not look down at those who have fallen even into major sins, it may be that Allah has chosen to humble them so that they repent to Him and beware of falling into false safety, for your deeds without the mercy of Allah can easily be wiped away.'

Abu Ayyub

'Do not look down at those who are not in the fold of your faith for it may be that one day, they will be your replacement.'

Abu Ayyub

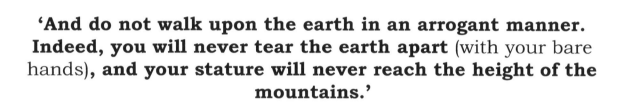

'And do not walk upon the earth in an arrogant manner. Indeed, you will never tear the earth apart (with your bare hands), and your stature will never reach the height of the mountains.'

The Sacred Qur'an 17:37

'Sometimes God breaks you in order to make you..'

Abu Ayyub

'Sometimes we have to be broken in order to be fixed.'

Abu Ayyub

'Every scar holds its wisdom'

Attullah

'Afflictions descend when ingratitude is rife.'

Abu Ayyub

'If you knew Allah as He should be known, you would leave people aside and take Him as your Companion.'

Ibn Al Qayyim

'Be to God as He wishes, and He will be to you more than you can wish for.'

Ibn Al Qayyim

'O you who are patient! Bear a little more, just a little more remains.' –

Ibn Al Qayyim

'If the human knew the pleasure of meeting Allah and being near to him, then he (the human) would feel grief for being distant from Him (Allah).'

Ibn Al Qayyim

'Our life in this world is like that of a harvest field. What you plant here is what you will eat in the hereafter.'

Abu Ayyub

'A sign of well being and success is that when one increases in knowledge, he becomes more humble and merciful.'

Ibn Al Qayyim

'The soul will never become pious and purified except through undergoing afflictions. It is the same as gold that can never be pure except after removing all the base metals in it.'

Ibn Al Qayyim

'When someone offends me, I think it's a gift from God. He is teaching me humility.'

Shaykhul Islam Ibn Taymiyyah

'As I look back on my life, I realize that every time I thought I was being rejected from something good; I was actually being re-directed to something better. You must convince your heart that whatever God has decreed is most appropriate and most beneficial for you.'

Imam Ghazali

'Every punishment from Him is pure justice and every blessing from Him is pure grace.'

Shaykhul Islam Ibn Taymiyyah

'Whoever wrongs you and then comes in order to apologize then you should accept his apology out of humbleness and leave his intention up to God, exalted is He.'

Ibn Al Qayyim

'O people who take pleasure in a life that will disappear; falling in love with a fading shadow is pure stupidity.'

Ibn Al Qayyim

'I'm trying to think, don't confuse me with facts.'

Plato

'It always seems impossible until it's done.'

Nelson Mandela

'Guidance is not attained except with knowledge and correct direction is not attained except with patience.'

Shaykhul Islam Ibn Taymiyyah

'The devil will always attack from two angles
Neglect and extremity, if he can push you to extremity and
burn you out then he will usher you towards neglect, and if
he panics you from neglect to extremity, he will attempt to
incite you to despair of the mercy of Allah.'

Abu Turab

'There is no changing of condition movement or might except in God Almighty.'

The Prophet Muhammad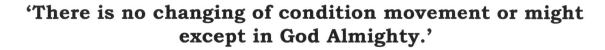

'I can by my own self do nothing'

Prophet Jesus in John 5:30

'I am a servant of God.'

Prophet Jesus in The Sacred Qur'an 19:30

'**He** (Jesus) **said: "I am a servant of God. He has given me The Book, and has made me a prophet.'**

The Sacred Qur'an 19:30

'Fellow Israelites, listen to this: Jesus of Nazareth was a man accredited by God to you by miracles, wonders and signs, which God did among you through him, as you yourselves know.'

Acts 2:22

'You should not honour men more than truth.'

Plato

'Indeed, God is The Truth.'

The Sacred Qur'an 22:6

'A winner is a dreamer who never gives up...'

Nelson Mandela

'Resentment is like drinking poison and then hoping it will kill your enemies.'

Nelson Mandela

'When the debate is lost, slander becomes the tool of the loser.'

Socrates

'Knowledge without action is vanity, and action without knowledge is insanity.'

Imam Ghazali

'Whoever prefers God to all others, God will prefer him to others.'

Ibn Al Qayyim

'I am not a saint, unless you think of a saint as a sinner who keeps on trying.'

Nelson Mandela

'The hypocrite looks for faults; the believer looks for excuses.'

Imam Ghazali

'To get what you love, you must first be patient with what you hate.'

Imam Ghazali

'Advice is easy, what is difficult is accepting it, for it is bitter in taste.'

Imam Ghazali

'Imam Ghazali was asked, 'What is the ruling of the one who left prayer?' He replied, 'The ruling is for you to take them along with you to the mosque.' Be a caller, not a judge.'

Imam Ghazali

'The measure of a man is what he does with power.'

Plato

'You are God's creatures so you should take heed of what He says...'

Abu Ayyub

'The price good men pay for indifference to public affairs is to be ruled by evil men.'

Plato

'As I walked out the door toward the gate that would lead to my freedom, I knew if I didn't leave my bitterness and hatred behind, I'd still be in prison.'

Nelson Mandela

'When men speak ill of thee, live so as nobody may believe them.'

Plato

'Lead from the back — and let others believe they are in front.'

Nelson Mandela

'Only the dead have seen the end of war.'

Plato

'A tyrant must put on the appearance of uncommon devotion to religion.[32] Subjects are less apprehensive of illegal treatment from a ruler whom they consider god-fearing and pious. On the other hand, they do less easily move against him, believing that he has God on his side.'

Aristotle

---

[32] Even if that religion be atheism or some political ideology, for indeed they are ways of life.

'Half of disbelief in God in the world is caused by people who made religion look ugly due to their bad conduct and ignorance.'

Imam Ghazali

'Ignorance is the root and stem of every evil.'

Plato

'Verily the soul becomes accustomed to what you accustom it to. That is to say: what you at first burden the soul with becomes nature to it in the end.'

Imam Ghazali

'Do not allow your heart to take pleasure with the praises of people nor be saddened by their condemnation.'

Imam Ghazali

'Misdeeds stand as a block for earning. Surely, one can be deprived of provision by committing sins.'

Ibn Al Qayyim

'Allah is displeased when you stop asking him and mankind is displeased when asked.'

Ibn Al Qayyim

'Prayer is one of the most beneficial form of medicine.'

Ibn Al Qayyim

'What is destined will reach you, even if it be beneath two mountains.
What is not destined will not reach you, even if it be between your two lips.'

Imam Ghazali

'The tongue is very small and light but it can take you to the greatest heights and it can put you in the lowest depths.
Soft words soften the hearts that are harder than rock, harsh words harden hearts that are softer than silk.'

Imam Ghazali

'The heaviest penalty for declining to rule is to be ruled by someone inferior to yourself.'

Plato, The Republic

'Dealing with people with kind words is perhaps dearer to them than offering them food and money to them.'

Ibn Rajab

'The bodies of the righteous are in this dunya, (this lowly world) but their hearts are connected to the hereafter'

Ibn Rajab

'Good manners are part of heedfulness and you cannot have heedfulness without good manners.'

Ibn Rajab al-Hanbali

'To completely trust in God is to be like a child who knows deeply that even if he does not call for the mother, the mother is totally aware of his condition and is looking after him.'

Imam Ghazali

'Wealth and children are only the beautification of this worldly life, but enduring good deeds are better with your Lord in terms of reward and better for one's hope.'

The Sacred Qur'an 18:46

'The one who is [truly] imprisoned is the one whose heart is imprisoned from Allah and the captivated one is the one whose desires have enslaved him.'

Shaykhul Islam Ibn Taymiyyah

'If you do not taste the sweetness of an action in your heart, suspect it, for the Lord, Exalted is He, is the Appreciative.'

Shaykhul Islam Ibn Taymiyyah

'The Messenger of God, peace and blessings be upon him, said, 'The word of wisdom is the lost property of the believer. Wherever he finds it, he is most deserving of it.'

The Prophet Muhammad ﷺ

'The heart on its journey towards Allah the Exalted is like that of a bird. Love is its head, and fear and hope are its two wings. When the head is healthy, then the two wings will fly well. When the head is cut off, the bird will die. When either of two wings is damaged, the bird becomes vulnerable to every hunter and predator.'

Ibn Al Qayyim

'When my servant asks about Me, then I am near, I respond to the one who prays when they pray, so they may respond to Me and believe in Me that thus they will be guided .'

2:186 The Sacred Quran

'Live in the way you want to die, for you will die in the way that you live.'

Abu Ayyub

'The people of Quran are those who read it and act upon it, even if they have not memorized it.'

Ibn Al Qayyim

'In life there is death and in death there is life.'[33]

Abu Ayyub

---

[33] The meaning is two-fold, in life we will die but also too much remembrance of the worldly affairs causes death to the spiritual heart, and in death there is life, again the meaning is two-fold, the hereafter starts with death, and so there is life in death, and the remembrance of death brings life to the heart.

'Whoever desires everlasting bliss, let him adhere firmly to the threshold of servitude.'

Shaykhul Islam Ibn Taymiyyah

For if we do then the following will be said to us:

'Peace be upon you for what you endured with perseverance, thus excellent is your final home.'

The Sacred Qur'an 13:24

'Whoever God wants good for He gives them understanding of the faith.'

The Prophet Muhammad ﷺ

Printed in Poland
by Amazon Fulfillment
Poland Sp. z o.o., Wrocław
01 May 2023

dbaed049-9406-4cff-9d2a-a0b84faa0d45R01